MW00412173

Opus Magnificat

1 Cancer Diagnosis.
24 Friends.
Magnificent.

Jennifer Tirrell Roberts

Foreword by David M. O'Donnell

Krista,
With love,
jennifer

CROSSBOOKS
PUBLISHING

CrossBooks™
A Division of LifeWay
1663 Liberty Drive
Bloomington, IN 47403
www.crossbooks.com
Phone: 1-866-879-0502

©2011 Jennifer Tirrell Roberts. All rights reserved.

*No part of this book may be reproduced, stored in a retrieval system, or transmitted
by any means without the written permission of the author.*

First published by CrossBooks 7/15/2011

ISBN: 978-1-4627-0541-2 (sc)

Library of Congress Control Number: 2011934065

Printed in the United States of America

This book is printed on acid-free paper.

*Certain stock imagery © Thinkstock.
Any people depicted in stock imagery provided by Thinkstock are models,
and such images are being used for illustrative purposes only.*

*Scripture quotations taken from the Holy Bible, New Living Translation, copyright 1996, 2004.
Used by permission of Tyndale House Publishers, Inc., Wheaton, Illinois 60189. All rights reserved.*

Scripture taken from the King James Version of the Bible.

*Scripture taken from the New King James Version. Copyright 1979, 1980, 1982
by Thomas Nelson, inc. Used by permission. All rights reserved.*

*Scripture quotations in this publication are taken from The Message. Copyright (c) by Eugene H. Peterson
1993, 1994, 1995, 1996, 2000, 2001, 2002. Used by permission of NavPress Publishing Group.*

*Scripture taken from the Holy Bible, New International Version®. Copyright © 1973,
1978, 1984 Biblica. Used by permission of Zondervan. All rights reserved.*

*Scripture taken from the Amplified Bible, Copyright © 1954, 1958, 1962,
1964, 1965, 1987 by The Lockman Foundation. Used by permission.*

*Scripture taken from the New Century Version. Copyright © 2005
by Thomas Nelson,Inc. Used by permission. All rights reserved.*

*Scripture quotations taken from the 21st Century King James Version®, copyright © 1994.
Used by permission of Deuel Enterprises, Inc., Gary, SD 57237. All rights reserved.*

*Because of the dynamic nature of the Internet, any web addresses or links contained in
this book may have changed since publication and may no longer be valid. The views
expressed in this work are solely those of the author and do not necessarily reflect the views
of the publisher, and the publisher hereby disclaims any responsibility for them.*

In memory of Debra S. O'Donnell

April 2, 1961–October 30, 2010

"As for me my life has already been poured out as an offering to God. The time of my death is near. I have fought the good fight, I have finished the race, and I have remained faithful. And now the prize awaits me—the crown of righteousness, which the Lord, the righteous judge, will give me on the day of his return. And the prize is not just for me but for all who eagerly look forward to his appearing."

2 Timothy 4:6–8

"Faith Eclipses Fear"

Foreword

by David M. O'Donnell

Debbie and I had twenty-three years of dating and marriage in total, and as most relationships go, there were highs and lows. What stands out most in my mind are not those highs and lows, but our commitment to each other to always stay together and never be low at the same time. Debbie always encouraged me that we would be fine in our marriage as long as when one was low the other one didn't go there with them. Because of this dogged determination by Debbie and I, we were able to navigate through the lows and truly embrace and welcome the highs. Over the years of our life together we created many friendships and maintained those friendships throughout the years. One of the incredible gifts of those friendships is illuminated in this amazing eclectic group of women in Deb's Bible study.

Going back almost two years now, I can't forget Debbie's exuberance as she came home from her first Bible study when she notified the Bible study of this new challenge: breast cancer. Debbie was extremely animated about this godly group of women who were going to help us through our many challenges to come. As most husbands do, I smiled and agreed with Deb, but in the back of my mind I honestly thought "What could twenty-three strangers do for my family now?" Wow, did I ever underestimate the power of twenty-three Christian women with a cause. I could recount the last eighteen months and the various random acts of kindness, but feel it's best to summarize the love and faith shared by these women in the following way.

One of the many blessings that my family received from the Bible study women was the willingness to relocate the meetings to our home. You see, I never would have been able to interact with the group, nor would have my children if the meetings stayed at Linda's home. To see Debbie "come alive" when they all walked in the house after having spent days before in bed or in agony from the pain, suddenly able to cope at such a higher level. This doesn't happen because of inner *strength*—it happens because of inner *faith, shared* amongst godly women. This lift in Debbie's spirit would have meant everything, but compound that with listening to these women sing hymns, sharing verses in the Bible and breaking out in hysterical laughter, and it literally reminded me of a group of angels. I now understood exactly why Debbie showed such exuberance about being supported by this group. I would be remise if I didn't mention the dozens of meals, rides for the kids, vacation homes offered and shared, and true friendships that were built. The real blessing came from the life long friendships that have been developed as these women entered my home week after week.

I have said many times that Debbie's gift to me is that she taught me how to live life, taught me how to laugh, and in the end taught me how to die … and now I can truly say another gift is the friendships of her Bible study women.

Acknowledgments

To my parents, Bud and (sister) Sally Fay, who adopted me, and then dedicated their lives to raise me after our parents died. Thank you for your example of sacrificial love through Christ.

Linda Goehle and Kirsten Locke read this memoir first. You inspired confidence in me. Thank you. I would also like to thank Chris Samoiloff for her photography expertise and generous heart to share it.

This memoir would not have been written without the encouragement of my study sisters. To them this message:

"xoxo Hugs <3".

Chapter One

"For our comely parts have no need: but God hath tempered the body together, having given more abundant honour to that part which lacked. That there should be no schism in the body; but that the members should have the same care one for another. And whether one member suffer, all the members suffer with it; or one member be honoured, all the members rejoice with it. Now ye are the body of Christ, and members in particular (1 Corinthians 12:24–27, KJV.)

"The way God designed our bodies is a model for understanding our lives together as a church: every part dependent on every other part, the parts we mention and the parts we don't, the parts we see and the parts we don't. If one part hurts, every other part is involved in the hurt, and in the healing. If one part flourishes, every other part enters into the exuberance" (1 Corinthians 12:25–26, The Message.)

It was October 2009. I drove to Linda's house, excited to begin a new adventure with God through our women's Bible study. We were studying *The Relationship Principles of Jesus* by Tom Holladay. As I arrived and helped Linda prepare for the women, we joyfully anticipated their happy voices. At six o'clock, all the beloved women streamed in, and we greeted each one with a hug. Soon, like always, the happy voices were all gathered in the kitchen as we caught up on each other's lives and ate delicious food: soups and stews, apple crisp, and all the fall favorites that taste especially good after the summer is past and the air is full of the wonderful, brisk coolness that indicates winter is on the way. We were energized about our new study and what God had in store for us in the coming months. What none of us realized was that His plan would cause us to come together as the body of Christ in a deeper, more challenging way than we ever imagined at that moment.

As the "facilitator" of these studies, I am often called upon to organize and lead the group. This is my pleasure, and a gift that the Lord has graciously bestowed upon me, whether I like it or not. I never cared for the gift of organization and always dreamed of having the gift of mercy, or teaching, or … oh … so many other gifts that I thought were more appealing. I remember the first time I did a spiritual gifting quiz during an adult Sunday school lesson. My first gift totaled up as "faith." I was happy with this conclusion! My next two gifts were "administration" and "organization." What? Those gifts just seemed so boring, but deep down I knew it to be true. How did faith and organization come together? I had no clue. I resentfully accepted the results of the "quiz."

Fast forward many years later, and picture me—a woman who at one point thought leading could be dull—herding a gaggle of women up the stairs and into our study room. It took time, but I not only accepted my gifts, but also learned to appreciate them and use them to the glory of God. It turns out that the gifts of faith and organization can work together beautifully in planning mission trips and all kinds of other events and studies. Praise His holy name. If left to my own devices, I'd still be wallowing in self-pity. Providentially, our loving Father not only imparts our gifts, but enables us to learn, grow, and understand how to use them as we incline our hearts and ears unto His voice.

Speaking of gifts, generosity and hospitality are two huge blessings that my co-facilitator possesses. Linda opens her beautiful home to us week after week. She is a widow, her husband having tragically been killed in a motor vehicle accident seven years ago. Raising three boys alone, she has kept her eyes focused on Almighty God, and He has been her rock and redeemer. She has used everything the Lord has blessed her with to bless the community around her many times over. Her home is "home" to all of us.

As inviting as Linda's kitchen is, the women eventually tore themselves away from the snacks, made it up the stairs, and settled in to begin our study. In walked Deb—our tall, gorgeous model/runner friend, her beautiful smile in place. She apologized for being late and plopped down on a chair.

Our first principle from *The Relationship Principles of Christ* by Tom Holladay was entitled: "Place the Highest Value on Relationships." This verse from Mark 12:29–31 NCV started our study:

Jesus answered (the teacher of the law). "The most important command is this: 'Listen, people of Israel! The Lord our God is the only Lord. Love the Lord your God with all your heart, all your soul, all your mind, and all your strength.' The second command is this: 'Love your neighbor as you love yourself.' There are no commands more important that these."

John Lennon wrote, "Life is what happens to you while you're busy making other plans." We had a plan in mind for study that evening, but we soon found out that God had a different plan for us.

Chapter Two

"As the heavens are higher than the earth, so are my ways higher than your ways and my thoughts than your thoughts" (Isaiah 55:9.)

When we gathered that October evening, ready to embark on our newest study with the Lord, we had no idea how radically changed we would become by October of 2010, a mere year later. We began study with prayer, asking that God would not only teach us the relationship principles outlined in Mr. Holladay's book, but that these principles would become real in our lives. We asked to be changed, really changed, as we studied the Jesus Creed: Love God and love others.

After the prayer time, our beautiful runner friend asked if she could share something. I looked over at "our Deb." At forty-eight years old she was stunningly beautiful; tall, thin, dark, and with a smile that was contagious. She coached the junior high school track team, ran a business from home after giving up her financial planning career to raise her three children, and if that wasn't enough, she had also cared for twenty-three foster children over the years. She began by telling us she had just purchased a new jogging bra.

All you women readers know that exercise bras can be very uncomfortable if you don't have the right fit, and even sometimes when you do! This new bra was no exception. After she wrestled it over her head and wiggled it down over her chest, she felt uncomfortable. It just didn't fit right or feel right. Her life changed as she shifted it around to try different positions. Deb explained, "I felt a lump on my breast. A big lump." There was silence in the room. "Do you want to feel it?" she asked. "I think you all should feel it so you know what it feels like in case you ever find one."

This transparency that Deb embraced by immediately drawing us in with her on her new adventure of faith would be consistent in the coming year. We all agreed that it was a good idea for us to meet the newest member of our group: cancer.

One by one we touched the lump. It was hard and seemed huge to me. Of course, we plied her with questions. She answered every one matter-of-factly. She was shaking just a little, but her voice was strong as she told us the news. Her neighbor is her primary care doctor, and she had called her to come over and look at the breast. The doctor was very concerned and she had appointments scheduled. Wow. Our plans for that evening's study changed dramatically in those moments. We gathered around our friend Deb and prayed over every aspect of her body and her family. We had asked just moments before that we would be changed, really changed. Had God just answered our prayer in a way that we could never have imagined?

After returning home that evening, my mind racing, I opened our new book to Chapter One. The first sentence was this: "Relationships are painful. Relationships are wonderful. We all live in the drama that plays out between these two truths." The book went on to teach that nothing is more important than relationships. We were going to have a chance to learn more from the "relationship expert," Jesus Christ, through the next many months. A flutter of excitement, or perhaps of nervousness, or maybe a little of each flowed through my body. I am sure of God's faithfulness, but know that often that comes with pain on this earth as we choose to follow Christ with the fervent prayer of becoming even a tiny bit more like Him each day.

In the following months, Deb's prognosis went from bad to worse. Stage 2 and one lump went to Stage 3 and two lumps, one in the breast and one in the clavicle. Then came the really bad news: Deb's cancer was one of the most aggressive types. She was now classified as Stage 4 because a lump was discovered in the other breast, and it became clear that the cancer had metastasized. She began chemotherapy immediately, and that would be followed by a radical double mastectomy. As Deb put it "My husband says that 'I got the man and fed the kids: get rid of them.'" She was always keeping us laughing and upbeat even as the grim news kept getting grimmer.

Despite the increasingly bad news, in the first few months that fall, there was a surety that all would be well. Surely this vibrant, healthy woman would fight off this vicious foe. We rallied around her, praying and bringing meals to the family on the chemotherapy days. Deb showed up for study more often than not, and we were privy to the most intimate details of her journey. This journey and our relationship journey went along hand-in-hand. God was giving us a wonderful opportunity to go from the "knowing" to the "doing." We knew that God places the most value on relationships, but actually walking this out in all aspects of our lives was wherein the challenge lay.

Chapter Three

"If you are looking for an adventure, you'll find it in having the faith to put your relationships first." —Tom Holladay

We had a hat and earring fashion show each Monday as Deb continued her chemotherapy treatments. All of us women had to step up our game on Mondays because it just wasn't right that the chemo patient looked better than the rest of us "healthy" women! I remember rejoicing at every report that the cancer was being beaten back, the tumors were shrinking on schedule, and Deb's competitive spirit was strong and in full attack-mode. Out went the sugary treats and junk food on study night, and in came fresh fruit and incredibly delicious vegetable concoctions. This was quite an adventure in and of itself; believe me! We treated ourselves and each other to all kinds of juices; beet and apple, carrot and garlic … you name it, in went the fruit and veggies and out came the juice. Some of us actually had to plug our noses to get it down, but we did it in the name of health! The body of Christ came together in these little ways in the beginning months. Wearing pretty earrings and changing our snack diet might not seem like much, but I believe we were like music students learning the first notes in a surprise symphony. God was gently tuning each of us as we submitted to His teaching.

Wikipedia defines piano tuning as the following: "Piano tuning is the act of making minute adjustments to the tensions of the strings of a piano to properly align the intervals between their tones so that the instrument is in tune. The meaning of the term in tune in the context of piano tuning is not simply a particular fixed set of pitches. Fine piano tuning requires an assessment of the interaction among notes, which is different for every piano, thus in practice requiring slightly different pitches from any theoretical standard."

While the women in our group fought their own particular battles on the home front; broken sibling relationships, trouble with husbands, struggles with children, and other difficult trials, we were able to all come together united as the body of Christ through Deb's battle. Our individual sufferings were no less painful than any pain she was experiencing: after all, suffering is suffering. I picture God seeing us as the individual strings on the piano, each different and requiring slightly different tones, and in His goodness and mercy, making the minute adjustments necessary to bring us into tune. He is doing this still. We claimed Philippians 4:8 as one of the most powerful verses in the Bible for fine-tuning our thoughts.

"Finally, brothers, whatever is true, whatever is noble, whatever is right, whatever is pure, whatever is lovely, whatever is admirable—if anything is excellent or praiseworthy—think about such things."

To have the faith to put all of our relationships first, ahead of our own desires, ahead of our faulty past thinking, ahead of the worldly standards and our prior childhood "programming," we would have to cling to this verse, as well as many others. "For the word of God is full of living power. It is sharper than the sharpest knife, cutting deep into our innermost thought and desires. It exposes us for what we really are" (Hebrews 4:12). The struggles we are were facing individually and corporately could only be conquered with the living power that comes from God's Word. We were in the thick of the battle! As Deb prepared for her radical double mastectomy, we were challenged by Holladay to love as Jesus loved. He put it as a "do more than you possibly could" challenge. To accept this challenge would mean trusting in Him alone.

It was about this time that Deb began to open up to me more about her past. I had only known her for a couple years, and most of that time it was on our Monday night study times. We had never really gotten a chance to delve into our pasts in a deep way. It takes time to really get to know a person, and being busy mothers of three kids each (we both had daughters that were high school freshmen and seniors, and I had an older son, she a younger son) we still had a lot to discover about one another. She began to tell me that she had been married for a couple years and divorced in her twenties, and so had I. She mentioned she and her husband had been married nineteen years, and so had my husband and I! We both grew up on lakes in upstate New York, as well. We made our baked beans the same way, we made our macaroni salad the same way, and we looked forward to salt potatoes every summer and even shared the same Blueberry Buckle recipe. We looked at each other and smiled, marveling that God had put us together "For such a time as this" (Esther 4:14). Our lives were so similar!

She had an idea for a Bible study. Wouldn't it be neat to go back in our lives and write down our history for the future generations to learn from? Why we made the decisions we did at that time, and was God working in any visible way as we made them? Did we pray? Did we believe? Did we hear His voice and ignore it to go our own way? Did we follow His voice, and what was the result? I agreed this would be a really good thing to do "some day." By fall of 2010, we were to make this vision a reality.

Chapter Four

"God has given gifts to each of you from his great variety of spiritual gifts. Manage them well so that God's generosity can flow through you. Are you called to be a speaker? Then speak as though God himself were speaking through you. Are you called to help others? Do it with all the strength and energy that God supplies. Then God will be given glory in everything through Jesus Christ. All glory and power belong to him forever and ever. Amen." 1 Peter 4:10–11 (NLT)

Deb never skipped a beat. On her way into surgery, her husband, Dave, reported that she even had the surgeons laughing with her. "I have a couple of things I need to get off my chest," she remarked. This healthy attitude might have had something to do with her speedy recovery. She was in Bible study the following Monday after surgery. No hair, but a cute hat … and of course, gorgeous dangly earrings and a fabulous matching necklace. No boobs, but a stylish blouse. As was customary, she somehow looked better than the rest of us. This, I believe, is a real testimony to the power of a positive attitude anchored in Christ. Not only was Deb's attitude excellent, but she was also realistic at the same time. Her surgery was in late February. We had planned a retreat at my home on Cape Cod the first weekend in March. Deb was hoping to make it to the retreat. Realistic? If you knew Deb, you would say "yes." Deb was *hoping* to make it to the retreat, but realized that she just couldn't do it. She needed to rest and heal.

We had chosen the "retreat in a box" entitled *Loving Well* by Beth Moore as our retreat study. We felt that this fit in wonderfully well with our current study of The Relationship Principles of Jesus. The Body of Christ is so vast. We studied under four different teachers during the year, and were awed by the way our God used them all to lead and guide us with their particular insight at just the right moment, all year through. It was Beth Moore's turn. (Beth, we feel we are good friends like you refer to us in your DVDs, so can I call you by first name?) Many of us have studied under Beth for many years through her DVD series. In the introduction to *Loving Well* she says "God had been dealing with me about loving people. He kept bringing me back to 1 John 4:7–8, AMP: Beloved, let us continue to love one another, for love is (springs) from God and he who loves (his fellowmen) is begotten (born) of God and is coming (progressively) to know and understand God (to perceive and recognize and get a better and clearer knowledge of Him). As I prepared, God spoke to me about the four kinds of people we studied that weekend. Some are easy to love. Some are difficult to love, and some are humanly impossible to love. God wants to demonstrate His *might* by doing through us what we cannot possibly do on our own. He wants us to learn to love all of these kinds of people—and love them well." This was exactly what we needed to learn as we dove deeper into the relationship principles and sought to apply them to our lives. The picture that Beth painted of Al*might*y God doing things through us, what we could not possibly do on our own, struck a cord deep in my heart. My prayer as we started planning the retreat was something like this: "Oh Lord! You sent your only son to die for us. How marvelous, how wondrous, how majestic is your name in all the earth. That you love us that much ... and now ... through that love we might be able to love others, even those seemingly impossible to love ... I just thank you so much. Teach us, Lord. Change us, Lord."

A leadership team was assembled. A group of us prayed and studied the material as we prepared to lead the small groups. A couple women worked on the skits and little gifts we planned to give each woman as she arrived. They also planned our "late night fun" that is so necessary for a women's retreat! Our talented friend Kirsten would be our worship leader. As I'm writing this, I'm picturing all the women's ministries across the globe that have planned retreats. I feel so connected to you all in such a heartwarmingly beautiful way. I've always thought that God's people are the most beautiful, talented group of individuals. Just as the individual instruments sound beautiful alone, when they all begin to play the piece together the music swells and surges to become divine.

Twenty-seven women signed up for the retreat. Thankfully, we have a spacious home on Cape Cod, and with women willing to bring air mattresses and blankets for themselves, we were all able to find a corner to call our own. On Friday the leaders carpooled to the coast together. We had such a tender time praying together for each dear, precious woman that was to attend and for those who couldn't make it. We had our nametags and welcoming gifts ready to go. Our skit was prepared (well, sort of ... our two talented ladies Sybil, aka Alice, and Dr. More or Less, aka Christine, were improvisation experts.) Alice acted out the four types of love in the well-known character of multiple-personalitied "Sybil." Dr. More or Less was Sybil's therapist. Those women did a fantastic job and had us cracking up before each DVD lesson began. The worship was moving, the lessons were deep, and the small groups began to share even more deeply.

As the weekend passed, we missed "our Deb" all the more. One creative participant suggested each small group come up with a "rap" during late night fun that we could video tape and play for Deb when we got home. We had had our pajama parade Friday night, and the five lucky winners received a chair massage by Dr. More or Less, our friend Christine, who also is a much-sought after massage therapist, even working for the Bush family in their Maine compound! The parade was very competitive, as you can imagine! We even had improvised talents thrown in for those who feared their pajamas alone wouldn't get them the prize. From high kicks to tap dancing, the women were outdoing each other. Did I mention that God's people are the most beautiful, talented people as far as I can tell? It was hard to surpass that pajama parade, but God surely blessed Cheryl's rap-for-Deb suggestion! Each group came up with the funniest, sweetest blessing-raps that you could possibly imagine. We had a ball rehearsing and taping the raps. We shared the DVD with Deb when we returned. Deb laughed, cried, and felt so much a part of the weekend after watching them.

Deb's incision was healing. How did we know? She showed her chest to us. With the same love as she had shown us by letting us feel her lump, she bared her disfigured chest to those she trusted. It is hard to put into words what it feels like to be a woman and look upon another woman who has been mutilated in this way. It was beautiful. It was tragic. It was heart wrenching. It was hard to see. A long, straight incision from one side of her body to the other was slashed across her flesh. It looked like it was healing well. She didn't even need any special bandages. She didn't bother with padding; she just wore pretty blouses that tied in the front, or had a lot of color and pattern to them.

Deb was in training for the Avon Walk for Breast Cancer. She was walking six miles each day, working up to the thirty-nine-mile, two-day walk. Around this time, I decided to have an *Anne of Green Gables* movie night at my home for those whom had never seen this childhood favorite. Several women brought their daughters over to see the first DVD. Everyone was wearing her pajamas because we figured we'd be cozier that way during the film. Deb arrived with her daughter Shannon in Linda's car. She came in through our backyard gate, around the pool to the back door. "I think I'll have everyone up to my cabin," she said as she dreamily looked down at the water. "We go skinny dipping every year. We all close our eyes while we undress, and then jump in!" She was pretty "loopy," having just had her meds upped, and she was having a great time already. I made two large bowls of popcorn and had some other sweets on hand. We made smoothies for anyone who wanted one. Naturally, Deb wanted a smoothie. She also liked the popcorn and the sweets. She was snuggled into the couch, chatting away through the whole movie. The popcorn bowl was propped beside her and she pretty much ate the whole thing while shooting off one question after the other to anyone within earshot. Even my husband, who came into the room to say hello, was bombarded with questions. By the end of the movie we thought she had exhausted herself … her stomach was definitely full (she had eaten all the popcorn, drank the smoothie, and had several handfuls of chocolate), and she had dozed off several times throughout the night. We were wrong. Again.

Deb was fearless and spontaneous her entire life. She made the most of every day. On her way back out by the pool, she announced she would go swimming. Linda, thinking to change her mind about that decision, said "You're not getting into my car with wet clothes!" Deb heard her and respected her decision. So, she promptly slipped out of her pajamas and underclothes and proceeded to wade in naked! I don't think I'll soon forget the look on my daughter's face as she watched that skinny body unabashedly walk into the pool without a care in the world! Thinking quickly, I said, "Let's *all* swim!" and dove off the diving board in my nightie. The water was surprisingly warm, and Deb and I floated around for a little bit, listening to the other women hoot and holler about our bravery to swim in New England in early May.

After receiving a towel to wrap herself up in on the way out of the pool, Deb mumbled, "Well, she *said* I couldn't get in the car with wet clothes …" We dissolved into peals of laughter again as we all shook our heads. What a woman.

Chapter Five

"Therefore, since we are surrounded by such a great cloud of witnesses, let us throw off everything that hinders and the sin that so easily entangles, and let us run with perseverance the race marked out for us." Hebrews 12:1

On May 15, Deb and a group of seventeen other "Princeton Warriors" began the Avon Walk for Breast Cancer in Boston, Massachusetts. The walking team was seventeen strong, but many people from the community came together to raise money as an outward sign of their support and love for the O'Donnell's and other cancer patients everywhere. Boston raised $5.8 million in the fight against cancer. Around $30,000 of it was from our community. The first day would finish after 26.2 miles. A marathon! Day two was a half marathon: 13.1 miles.

The Princeton Warriors began training in early spring, not long after Deb's surgery. Deb had been a coach for many years in the Princeton grade school, and the name of the school track team is the Princeton Warriors. The walking team figured that was a nice, strong fighting name as well. It was rare that Deb missed a practice walk, and she generally led the walkers with her strong, long-legged pace. Her chest might have been sore and her arm growing evermore useless, but "From my waist down, I'm still the same!" she would cheerfully remind us anytime she was asked how she was doing.

Her walking partners remember having some great conversations as they trained. God was in the conversations. It occurred to them that the *whole* time of Deb's sickness was all about people coming to know Christ, and for us that knew Him already, to grow more as His disciples.

The team decided to do a ladies pampering night to raise money for the walk. They had an awesome turnout. Deb was making beet juice shooters with her juicer, and Chris was making fruit smoothies with her blender. So many people volunteered services. Deb K. washed feet all night like Jesus had for His disciples. At one point a friend looked over and watched Deb K. ministering to people as she washed their feet, and she had to go quickly into the bathroom to compose herself; she was so touched it made her weep. Laurie was able to talk about God's love to the ladies while doing manicures and facials. I believe one of them said she wanted to start going back to church. Wonderful conversations were held with women who had battled breast cancer themselves. Not sure how much money this little venture would net, they were pleasantly surprised—they made $3,066! God was answering our prayers. His "calling cards" were everywhere! We were being changed by His love, and His love was drawing others, too.

I asked one of the walkers, Chris Samoiloff, a dear friend of Deb's and mine as well, to write her memories of the walk. Here is what she wrote:

"Deb, especially on the first day, set the pace. According to Tammy, at one point she and Andy were walking together and were trailing Deb. Andy asked Tammy if she wanted to catch up to Deb, and Tammy told Andy she was walking as fast as she could already.

I woke up the second day and told Andy I didn't think I could walk. A few of us felt that way. Deb was dizzy and went to the medical tent. We told her she shouldn't walk, but she didn't listen (*quelle surprise!*). Erika was sick (and walked sick the whole way) but she said if her mom could walk, she could walk. All of us walked that second day.

Deb didn't get any blisters. I got three of them. By the end of the walk it felt like knives were cutting into my feet with every step. When Deb and I walked four years ago for my sister-in-law, Laurel, she's the one that got the blisters and I didn't get any. I was happy to get them in her place this time around!

At the walk, they hand out ribbons that said "Every 3 minutes" on them. They signify a cancer diagnosis. If you are handed one, you are supposed to wear it for the remainder of the walk. When Deb and I walked for Laurel (again, she was several steps ahead of me) she got handed a ribbon. I caught up to her and said "Oh, Deb! It's one of those ribbons!" She had thought they were handing her a trash bag. We stopped right there and she said, "This is just how it would be in real life. You'd be going into a doctor's appointment for a normal physical and they'd come back and tell you the news." We both started crying. I told everyone at the beginning of the walk that this time that I wasn't accepting a ribbon if I got handed one. I avoided one the first day, but I woke up to one outside my tent. I told Dave's friend Mike the story about Deb getting handed the ribbon, and I told him I was planning on throwing this one in the trash. I asked him if he wanted it, and he said that he thought the trash was the perfect place for it.

When Tammy got handed a ribbon she said something like: "I'm not superstitious, and if I do get diagnosed with breast cancer, I hope I can handle it with the grace and dignity Deb is handling hers." Many of our group did get handed ribbons.

I was taking pictures along the way, and at one point Deb and Dave had stopped to pee in some bushes. It was a perfect photo opportunity, but I asked the people around me if I should take it (it was kind of a private moment) and Erika said, "Go for it." I love that picture. Deb saw me taking it and she has a cute little grin on her face.

I was walking with a friend, Bill, for a bit and he told me he didn't know he was walking all these miles until the week before. When he found out he asked his daughter if they couldn't find a shorter walk to do and she told him, "Dad, we're doing this." And so he did. What a trooper! He said it was a wonderful thing to do with his daughters, and he had some great father-daughter time.

At one point, Andy joked that if we signed up now for next year, we could get something like a $10 discount off of our registration fee. Bill said, "I think I'm going to work this year directly on finding a cure for cancer instead." The walk stirred a deeper commitment in Bill.

I was walking with Deb at one point, and I can't remember exactly what conversation led into this comment, but she said there would be plenty of time to rest, and that this (doing this walk) is what made her feel alive.

At the beginning of the walk, during the opening ceremonies, I was overwhelmed with emotion. I was glad that only Andy was with me at that point. Deb and I had walked for Laurel, and she had lost her battle with cancer. Now here we were walking for Deb, and there was a good chance she was going to lose her battle, too. After that, though, I was okay for the rest of the walk. Other people got emotional along the way as well.

Pam and Howard, Deb's dad and step-mom, joined us a few times along the way, including walking into the finish of the first day hand-in-hand with Deb and Dave. Precious. The beginning of the second day, Deb's son Parker was there along the route as a complete surprise for Deb, cheering her on—another really precious moment. At the finish line the second day, there were additional friends and family to welcome us in.

Dave ministered to a lady in a wheelchair who had advanced cancer. He helped her up over curbs; he walked with his hand on her shoulder for a bit. It was so beautiful.

I can't remember whom I was walking with, but we came on a bunch of buttons they were selling. One of them said "save second base." I (and whoever it was I was with) couldn't understand why they had something to do with Fenway Park at this event. Sure, we were in Boston, but why at the Avon Walk? Duh. We eventually figured it out. Parker has that button. I saw him wearing it the other day."

I just love Chris's reflections of the walk. The Avon Walk website challenges us to "alter the lives of thousands affected by breast cancer worldwide. Together, we will unite with one purpose and one goal—to end this deadly disease." This goes for all types of cancer. My father is a non-Hodgkin's lymphoma survivor of many years. I am exceedingly grateful for the research that went into his cure … and thankful for all the donations … and missing toenails … that make this research possible!

New relationships were developed throughout the two-day march. As bodies broke down from the exertion, spirits were stretched and strengthened in corresponding measure. Lives of thousands were "altered" by the way Deb, and others like her, were living out their faith during those two days. Deb shared her marvelous eternal perspective with anyone who would listen. She had approximately thirty-two hours to get her message out, and she did not waste one single minute of that time. Her bald head broke their hearts, her smile drew them in, and her conviction opened their eyes to see beyond the disease to the eternal.

In our study times, we were just finishing up *The Relationship Principles of Jesus*. In chapter 40, we were challenged with the question: "What would life look like if you began to live out in all your relationships with this kind of love Jesus taught?" It struck me that we had a pretty good idea now what it would look like … from watching Deb in action.

The O'Donnell family—Dave, Shannon, Erika, Deb, Parker
and foster daughter, Cassie

Deb and Dave during her chemo treatments.
(Chris Samoiloff photos)

Deb and Erika enter the Atlantic Ocean in Sarasota, FL
(Scot Loveless photo)

Some of the Bible study women at out summer study

The Avon Walk for Breast Cancer, May 2010
(Pam Loveless photo)

Deb with her "cute little grin."
(Chris Samoiloff photo)

Deb, Erika, and Shannon "cabin-hopping" in Sunapee, NH
(Linda Goehle photo)

Girls weekend at Deb's cabin in the Adirondacks

Erika's quilt made by Deb's Bible study ladies, her mom, and
step-mom Pam Loveless
(Linda Goehle photo)

Deb bundled up for an October canoe ride
(Linda Goehle photo)

God might give us a miracle,
but God might not.
And even then, He's still GOD,
and He's still SOVEREIGN,
and I will love Him
and worship Him
every day.

— Deb O'Donnell

A memorial to Deb
(Chris Samoiloff photo)

Chapter Six

"Pressed out of measure ..." (2 Cor. 1:8)

"That the power of Christ may rest upon me" (2 Cor. 12:9).

As a rule, when you are delivered the diagnosis of stage four metastasized cancer, the doctors give you up to a year to live regardless of what you try to do to change it. Deb had had a course of chemotherapy that shrunk the tumors significantly; she had changed her diet; she was receiving vitamin C treatments on a regular basis. She was now suffering the trauma to body and spirit that results from having your breasts removed. It was mid-winter on the calendar, and mid-winter in her soul. She began to realize that there were things she wanted to do before she died.

One day it was my turn to drive her to her vitamin C treatment. Her husband, Dave, had driven her to most of her treatments in the early months, but we insisted we would love to spend the time with Deb, and it was not an inconvenience. This relieved him, knowing she was in loving hands, and it enabled him to continue to run his business and get some much-needed time to do some of the things he loved to do. We fully understood how much he needed to stay healthy himself and find time to exercise and take care of the home. Both his parents and Deb's parents were pitching in on the home front, and between all of us we managed to keep smiling and get everything done that needed to be done. I had not yet driven Deb to a treatment, and I didn't really know what to expect. She lay down attached to the IV machine where the vitamin C slowly dripped into her system. Deb was healthy and had virtually no viruses or infections the entire fifteen months she was sick. We believe the vitamin C was integral in keeping her immune system strong.

Deb asked me to get a pen and paper one day when she decided she wanted to write her "bucket list." I have to tell you that my heart almost stopped when I heard that request. I thought "God? Are you *sure* I'm supposed to be right here, right now? Why me?" It was at that moment that I truly knew that yes, He had called me to be here beside Deb at this time. He knew that I would, with the gifts he had so graciously bestowed upon me, "get things done" on the list. It was difficult to grasp the magnitude of the moment, but, having a bias for action, I found the pen and paper and started writing.

Deb had a long list of prayers for salvation for those she loved. She had a "top ten list." Like many of us, she had led a different life before she became a devoted follower of Christ, and she was open and willing to share her past. Her teen years were unruly, and she ran away from home several times during those years. She was independent and strong, and eventually became a self-made businesswoman, working in the financial field and doing extremely well. She loved to travel and spend time with her family. She loved life and lived it to the fullest expression of how she knew life to be lived at that point. She married, and divorced. She worked with her husband, Dave, who asked her out approximately forty-nine times before she finally accepted a date. No one was more surprised than he was when she decided to stay home after their first daughter, Erika, was born. Their "miracle" daughter, Shannon Faith O'Donnell, followed Erika three years later.

Deb was in her first trimester with Shannon when she had her standard prenatal testing. She and Dave were shocked to learn that Shannon possessed the chromosomal abnormalities associated with Downs syndrome. Faced with this news, she and Dave turned to family, friends, and eventually to prayer to decide what to do. There were those who suggested abortion. There were those who shared the beauty and blessing of raising a Downs child. Both Dave and Debbie were talented athletes. As many parents do, they dreamed of the days when their children would join them in these activities and maybe excel at a sport and become an Olympic athlete. As they prayed and sought an answer, Dave became excited about the Special Olympics. He called Deb and said, "Let's do this," and they chose to have their baby.

The day came for Shannon's birth. The hospital room was specially prepared. Often Down's babies have multiple birth defects, and the hospital is ready to handle any surprises that might have been missed during the ultrasounds and other testing. No one was more surprised than the doctors, however, when Shannon was born. As they rushed her to the care station to inspect her closely, they found … well … nothing. She looked like a perfectly healthy newborn. Dave, peering around the nurses and doctors, prepared to love this little one no matter what, describes the time as "almost a disappointment"! Puzzled glances were followed by the news: Deb had given birth to a healthy, strong, baby girl. There is still no medical explanation. Shannon's health is a miracle: a gift from a God who loves us even before we love Him back. You see, Deb and Dave didn't really know to whom they were praying when they asked for His wisdom with their decision. They prayed in faith, and Faith became Shannon's middle name. Faith believes without seeing. God took that mustard seed of faith, and about eight years later, Dave and Deb asked Jesus to be their Savior. "Then Jesus told him, 'You believe because you have seen me. Blessed are those who believe without seeing me'" (John 20:29). Dave and Deb received another blessing two years later when their son, Parker, was born.

Driving Deb to her appointments was a blessing that we sisters all shared and enjoyed. During these drives we learned more about her and her life. Interestingly, though, it was Deb who grilled us about our lives the most. She would ask pointed and direct questions about our pasts, our husbands, our children and our faith. She wanted to really know us deeply. Our friend, Alexis Benander, told me she was in awe of Deb's candidness in regards to her past, her present, and her fear for her future. These are her words:

"I was the first of us girls to take her to her vitamin C infusion in Arlington. I didn't know what to expect, but she put me to ease immediately. I didn't need my GPS, as she had been with family and knew the way. She had asked me to talk about heaven. We shared what we thought it was like. She looked at it as a place of great wonder and peace. As she lay on the treatment table, she had me write out cards to each of her children that would be sent to them as they passed through milestones in their lives. She dictated and I wrote. I was always amazed at how the most wonderfully encouraging words just passed through her lips, and I knew that I was part of her gift of love to them. I was grateful. She had me seal these cards and write in small print where the stamp went and what the subject matter was. They were given to a relative to mail at their designated time. She asked me if I thought she was doing the right thing with these cards and journals, or if she would make it harder on her children. She knew I had lost my mom in my twenties and she wanted my insight. I told her that if I had a letter to me from my mom, I would to this day sit at times and re-read it over and over. This day she felt great nausea and almost needed to go to Mass General for treatment. They were able to give it to her there with the doctor's permission. On the way home she ate like a trooper, but was very tired.

The next treatment was the same—more cards. She would encourage me to go shopping or to lunch if she were to fall asleep during treatment. I would leave for a bit and come back with a chocolate shake for her. When I returned, she was usually on the phone with Parker giving instructions, or a on the phone with a doctor—but "never" asleep. And boy, she loved her chocolate shakes! This time on the way home we were discussing her cancer and treatment. She had me pull over to the side of the road and pulled down her dressing so I could see cancer in its advanced stage. She was so incredibly open. I admired her for it. She made me wonder if I would be able to do that, or if my pride would have prevented it. That's the day I learned that she was not prideful, and I loved her more. She was very tired and went straight to bed when she got home.

The next treatment was the same, but this time we went to Worcester (U Mass) for radiation. She would have me hold her wallet and cell phone; I knew she trusted me. She asked me to take her grocery shopping afterward, so we went to Price Chopper. Just as we entered I asked the manager if Deb could get my discounts from my card. She said "no," but she could fill out her information for a temporary card. As we shopped the manager found Deb and helped her fill out the card in the isle. When we went through the line the manager came over and told the bag boy to bring all of our bags out to the car. Deb said that was truly one of the best shopping experiences she had ever had, and we laughed. I couldn't believe she had pushed a full cart around the store with one arm. She had sure had drive! There was nothing wrong with her memory, either! She didn't buy tomatoes because we were going over to Chris S.'s house to get her garden tomatoes, but when we got home, Deb was tired; too tired to go gather tomatoes. As Parker and I brought in the bags, Deb excused herself and went to bed. I was tired myself and was trying to imagine how she had put so much energy into one day. Her drive never ceased to amaze me. I wanted to be just like her.

We went for a three-mile walk one day and talked a lot. We shared our pasts, all of the accomplishments and mistakes. She was not judgmental. She shared family secrets and I shared mine. She took me to her cemetery plot and showed me where the brook was and how she planted a bunch of lupine bulbs there so her family could find her more easily. She shared her disappointments. We discussed Dave re-marrying. She said she didn't want him to marry for at least four years. I asked if that was a bit unrealistic, but She said she didn't want any other woman raising Parker. She felt the girls were on their way, but he was still young. I tried to assure her that no woman could undo the mom she is in Parker. She had left her mark of love and character building in him by then and she didn't need to feel threatened. She would later share with me that this conversation brought her great peace. She made me feel like I was being used by God. I loved the way she made me feel. We both agreed that had we known each other longer, we would have always been great friends.

When I went to her house for the fundraiser, I marveled at her enthusiasm with the juicer. Her hope, her positivity, her energy, her being … it lifted my heart. I couldn't help but compare myself to her if in this position, and hoped I would be just like her! I've learned through her not to be afraid to ask for help. I never do. She showed me that needing help is not a weakness but a fact, and I need to let go of my pride. We all need each other's help at some point.

I was blessed beyond belief when she called me and invited me to her cabin that fall. I loved being part of her special girls get together. I still marvel at how she was able to pull this off. I saw her daughter be her caregiver and knew she was a great mom. I could see how special she had been for years with her friends from N.Y. She had a way of pulling people together in a big way. She was salvation-minded and on an agenda. Never pushy … always the "example." I was just looking at pictures of that weekend and I still can't believe it was only six weeks before her passing. It's surreal.

Deb allowed herself to be transparent to us all and we gained a lot from that. We walked through the valley of death with her and feared no evil. We were allowed to experience her journey through her eyes and heart. That is a gift that is rare. We've all seen *Scrooge* and know that death comes in the form of a big black, hooded, scary shape. To us it came with a beautiful face, the face of Deb O'Donnell and one that will be embraced."

You can see from Alexis' memories what a gift Deb's life was and how much we all learned as we walked the valley together. Deb's bucket list was not terribly long, and most of it was thinking ahead in ways to bless others, especially her family. Deb wanted to make a quilt for each of her children. She wanted to go to Nantucket. She prayed her son, Parker, would choose to be baptized. She prayed her children would be close forever and count on each other always. She wanted a summer Bible study. On the list was a special prayer for her pastor and his wife: that they would find relief and rest on their sabbatical. We cried together as we wrote the list. We still clung to the belief that all would be well, but deep down inside … when we looked into each other's eyes … we wondered if that meant all would be well with her soul as she went to be with Jesus, or if all would be well here on earth after she was physically healed. Either way, she had given the list to the right person. The next day I set out to "make things happen!"

Chapter Seven

"This I recall to my mind, therefore I have hope. Through the LORD's mercies we are not consumed, because His compassions fail not. They are new every morning; great is your faithfulness. The LORD is my portion," says my soul, "Therefore I hope in Him!" Lamentations 3:21–24

The Body of Christ came together. This is what it looked like with regard to the bucket list. I contacted Deb's friend who was already organizing the quilt project and volunteered our Bible study to help her. She used her quilting talent to instruct me as to what needed to be purchased, and we chose a time to meet. We would meet for an hour of study and then follow with an hour of quilt-making each week. I shot out an e-mail, and the sisters responded. We sang, prayed, and studied each week, and then we cut, ironed, and sewed together. We were led to read and study the psalms through David Jeremiah's book *When Your World Falls Apart: Seeing Past the Pain of the Present.* In the acknowledgments, Jeremiah says, "When I first encountered my bend in the road in the fall of 1994, I did not think I would write a book about my experience. But the lessons I learned have been too valuable to keep to myself. This is not primarily a story about me; it is a record of God's dealings with me during these traumatic years. As always, He works best through the people He brings next to us at such crucial times." We felt, and feel the same way. We just *must* share the beauty and wisdom gleaned from such experiences! I just must include some of the precious e-mails that share our hearts' journey this past summer, 2010. I hope they will bless you.

Dear Precious Sisters,

Today with Deb was wonderful as Jen led us in exploring Psalm 138. Following are some of the vital lessons we learned.

1. It is hard sometimes to love God with your whole heart. It is in times of suffering that it is made easier. 'In times of trouble the most clearly marked path to God is not the way of struggle and desperation but rather of worship.' David so clearly shows us this in this psalm and so many others.
2. It takes fortitude to open our eyes and see beyond that which has been taken away from us, which pales in comparison to what more we have to be grateful for. We must find reasons to thank God and things to be grateful for. Focusing on our misery only traps us in our own private dungeon.
3. I love this one. When David cried out to God, even as we do, he always received an infusion of renewed vitality to face the problems ahead of him.
4. We must bow in humble recognition of who we are and who God is. We sang 'your ways oh Lord are higher than our ways oh Lord and your thoughts are higher than our thoughts oh Lord.' We surrender the two-year-old in us who cannot understand multiplication any more than we can understand His ways and thoughts. He will continue to perfect us.

We prayed together, laying hands on Deb and anointing her with oil. We cried and rejoiced in His power and might. And our dear sister was renewed. I am grieved that I must now miss the next six or so lessons so I look forward to your reports. Please keep me in the loop. I shall miss you and the tender moments we share together. Love, Cindy

Hello Dear Women!

Sorry for this delayed update! I left the cape at 8 a.m. and am now back, stuffed with yummy pizza, and ready to write a recap of our precious study hours.

We began the study with worship and praise! We lifted our voices, praising Him for His amazing grace, and then went on to raise our song to "How Great Thou Art." After prayer, Deb shared her weekend in Maine with us. A great many of her extended family and several friends and their families gathered together for Independence Day. As Deb put it 'God was all over the weekend.' She cited many occasions where she felt His presence … one time when she was gathered with her brothers right before they were to leave the following morning, and they were hugging and crying. Gathered around were 10–15 other family members. She was able to let them know her surety of where she was going … and advised them that they need not fear ever being apart, if only they accepted the gift of salvation. Tears were shed amidst the stars that glorious evening. Her young twenty-one-year-old nephew helped her back to her cabin, wanting to spend more time with her. In the morning she found a long note where he shared that he knew God, but felt he didn't really 'know' Him. After witnessing Deb and her family, he wanted to know Him better. Deb promised she would give him practical ways to increase his faith and knowledge through the Bible, the Word. She then began daily contact with this precious soul. Another instance she shared was a couple in her family who was struggling in their marriage. The husband had become emotionally attached to a woman at work, and this was undermining his relationship with his wife and young children. After Deb shared with them (instructing the husband to break off the relationship completely) they cried, hugged one another, and hand-in-hand went back to their cabin. Praise God! Many wonderful weekend moments were expressed, and we could picture Deb swimming to the raft sidestroke … and one-handedly climbing the ladder. With a little nudge from a cousin or someone, up she went onto the raft! Another friend, Karen, expressed it best when she saw Deb today … in a gorgeous black sundress, eyeliner, lipstick and looking FINE … 'wow!'

Yes, we did move on to Psalm 63, but not before all of us had a chance to share what God had done in our lives during the very same weekend—I can't go into detail here without writing a book, but please know it was all wonderful. Omni-present. That's all I need say.

We started study reading from Cindy's fabulous outline of the chapter. A few tears were shed as we realized our 'gaping holes' and how we tend to fill it with the earthly things that just leave us feeling empty. We wondered why we don't go to His sanctuary as a rule, and fall back to these creature comforts that don't satisfy ... when we already *know* they *won't?* We discussed sin-consciousness vs. righteous-consciousness and were thankful to know Jesus' blood already covers *all* our past sins, present sins, and future sins. It is already *done.* He loves us just how we are and sees that we are grieved when we seek other comfort outside of Himself ... and knows our hearts. What a comfort!

We all agreed with both Cindy and Robin when they quoted 'holy, essential, and irreplaceable is the Spirit of God manifest among His people,' and we were so very thankful to have church families and unity among the brethren.

I could go on and on. We ended with a time of praise and prayer. Many tears were shed and knees hit the floor as we thanked Him for His mercy and grace, and for our Deb, for each other, our families, and new life to come in the form of grandchildren-to-be ... and oh-so many other praises! Almighty God is *good!* He is *faithful!* He is *all in all, Alpha and Omega* and *Emmanuel.* Love, Jennifer.

How I wished I could have been with you all today. Struggling through the questions of what God allows and what God causes. That's really tough stuff that we may never know the answers to this side of heaven, but some comfort I have found from my Beth Moore study of the book of Daniel is where she says, 'God abides with us, but we are wise to remember that His ultimate goal is for us to abide with Him. At some point, Beloved, you and I are going home. He alone knows how. Sometimes God delivers us from the trial. Other times He delivers us through the trial. Still other times He delivers us by the trial into His arms. What motivates the difference? Somehow and someway glory is at stake. Our God is able to deliver us. Every time! And how often He does! If ever He does not and the flames of death or tragedy consume us, it is to light a fire somewhere and in some heart that can never be extinguished. Trust Him to the death. Trust Him through the death. In the blink of an eye, we'll understand.' Beth goes on to say that there are three scenarios when we face trials: Scenario A: We can be delivered from the trial. Dividend? Our faith is built. Scenario B: We can be delivered through the trial. Dividend? Our faith is refined. Scenario C: We can be delivered by the trial into His arms. Dividend? Or faith is perfected. I pray that the Lord, through the power of the Holy Spirit, would infuse Deb and Dave with the courage to persevere and to remain faithful to God in this fiery trial and trust that God will be glorified in and through this battle with cancer, and that if it is His purpose and plan to deliver Deb by this trial into His loving arms, that we will all be comforted by the knowledge that we will one day be reunited (and what a Bible study we will have in heaven), and that we will together praise and worship God for all eternity! May God bless you, bring you peace and comfort as we continue to support and encourage Deb and one another through this fiery trial.

Love, Robin

Deb's friend Vivian made the front of the first quilt. Those of us that were quilting-challenged ironed fabric and cut out old memory t-shirts that the kids had chosen to include on the back of the quilt. One talented friend, Chris, used her computer skills to copy Scriptures the kids had chosen and created iron-on transfers. Deb's mom Pam assembled the back of the quilt. All our talents combined to make the job easy and fun! The relationships that grew from working together were precious. While we sewed and ironed, we talked and shared. Our love for each other grew. We all had personal struggles, and we all had moments of pain as we remembered why we were making the quilts, but greater than those things was the joy we all shared through knowing Christ. God's own blanket of peace settled on us as we created those quilts for Deb's children.

Deb's parents had gotten divorced when she was a child, and she loved both sets of parents dearly. They took turns helping the family, two to three weeks at a time, during her illness. Depending on which Mom was visiting, they joined in with us! We loved getting to know them all, and over time, they became like family to us as well. Deb was fond of saying how much she loved them all … and how what had seemed like a tragedy upon hearing her parents would divorce, soon became a blessing as she allowed herself to be loved by her wonderful new step-parents. Every Bible study, and every time she spent time with each of us, Deb would be sure to tell us how thankful she was and that she "loved us so much."

I began making plans to make her Nantucket wish come true. Here is a copy of an e-mail I sent to our sisters. It pretty much tells the story of what happened that bucket list weekend.

> Hi all!
>
> What a weekend we have had! So blessed and prayed over!
>
> Friday night they got here by 6—no traffic thanks to your prayers. Right away we all felt at home and enjoyed each other's company. We ate dinner and just gabbed until bedtime. Deb didn't sleep much, and frankly, neither did any adult for various reasons, but that didn't even matter. We were up early to catch the 8 a.m. ferry with smiles on our faces!
>
> We rented bikes … brave Deb and Dave tested a bicycle built for two and decided she could handle it so off we all went on bikes to the beach! God provided perfect weather! It was sunny, but with a fabulous breeze. We dug her a sand chair with an arm prop and plunked her in it. Parker set up her umbrella and *viola!* Paradise. The ocean waves, four gorgeous girls laughing and bonding, the guys took a jog and I cheerfully fussed over Deb determined to create the ultimate sand chair.
>
> After a few hours we headed back to the town and had a nice lunch. We shopped a bit and got on the ferry back.

Deb was beginning to have more pain at this point. After we got home, she took to her bed for a rest. The Doctor was called at about 6 so I went in and prayed and sang for a while. Then I had the girls come in. We prayed and sang and rubbed her everywhere we could. This was a very beautiful time together. Deb was granted relief from the pain somewhat! We got out Psalm 13 and studied together, reading from our book and the Bible. By 8 p.m. she was able to come out for dinner! Praise God!

We ate and played games together until 10:30 p.m.!

Today the men and Parker are heading over to MV on our boat for breakfast. Girls are sleeping in! Then golf for the three guys. We'll probably shop some more. Deb has something in mind to get.

We prayed thankfulness for our sisters. Deb said she knows God gave her us because she only has brothers and she needed sisters.

Love to you, Jennifer

Chapter Eight

"In contrast to happiness stands joy. Running deeper and stronger, joy is the quiet, confident assurance of God's love and work in our lives- that he will be there no matter what! Happiness depends on happenings, but joy depends on Christ." (Philippians NIV Chapter Introduction)

The trip to Nantucket kick-started what turned out to be a busy summer "cabin-hopping." After spending time at my cape house, we carved out a weekend at Linda's cabin on Perkins Pond in New Hampshire, and another in the Adirondacks, where the O'Donnells' cabin was located. A couple of things were consistent with each visit. We had to string up a chain to elevate Deb's arm while she slept so that the fluid could drain back down her arm during the night. Her arm would swell up during the day because of the removal of her lymph nodes, and during the night it would get "back to normal." We decided this was God's way of having her praise Him all night long ... even in her sleep her arm was lifted high in praise and thanks "in all circumstances."

Another consistent part of Deb's travels was the loving way her daughters, Erika and Shannon, cared for her. One or both of them was always with her. Even at the tender ages of eighteen and fifteen they would lovingly clean and bandage her wounds, compliment her, fix her hair, do her makeup, paint her toenails, and tuck her into bed in the evenings. It was a gift for my daughters to be able to witness their peers caring for their mom in this way. It was not easy to care for Deb at this point. She made it seem easy, however. The daily bandaging was quite complex. You see, she had developed skin cancer as well. The cancer was bulging through the incision on her chest, making that area very raw. The cancer had travelled down her left arm, making it mostly useless. And yes, she was left-handed.

Although the usage loss of this arm was extremely difficult for Deb to deal with, she fondly referred to it as "the claw."

I remember the day Deb asked me to learn how to dress her wound. (Me? Are you kidding? I don't have that gift, remember? But, okay, God … if you say so.) Upstairs I went. This particular day, Deb's mom was there and it was she that so tenderly showed me how to douse the wound with the anti-septic. The "wound" encompassed almost her entire chest area, and lay exposed and raw. It didn't match at all with "our Deb's" beautiful head and neck. It wasn't the first time I had seen it. In fact, I had seen it in every stage, from at first feeling the lump on her beautiful, smooth flesh, to the leathery radiation scabs, to what now was just oozing, raw flesh. We "wrapped" her in special bandages that went up around her shoulder and back around and around. We gently placed her underclothes over the bandages and then on came her lovely blouse, chunky necklace, and of course, matching earrings. Looking into her eyes, one found oneself having to pause and look deeply, with an unexplainable yearning … needing to spend a moment there, connecting with this … well … piece of eternity, I think, that was slowly revealing itself more and more in her the closer she came to it. You know, I never had to dress her much after that because her faithful daughters and loving parents were there to do it, and when they weren't able, sisters in our group that were nurses took over her care, but I am glad I got that opportunity to learn how, and to hold her hand as she blessed me yet again by insisting I come up and learn how beautiful it is to care for people we love in whatever way they need at a particular time. To not be afraid, but to trust Him as He leads us, wherever He leads us.

And lead us He did! My favorite times at our cabin-time in New Hampshire were the mornings. The three women would lay in a big bed and do our morning study with our coffee, listening to the men and the kids laughing as they took an early morning dip off the rope swing, or working together as they made our breakfast. Deb's arm was rigged up to a log beam overhead, and somehow it all seemed normal at this point. We rejoiced as her appetite returned, and she polished off plate after plate of food, and cheered as her body eliminated it on its own without meds. There was much hope in our hearts. I love Linda's remembrances from that time together:

"Our group was a wonderful combination of people who love to laugh, play, and share from their hearts … and we did it all. Bible studies together each morning on my bed for Deb, Jen and I; early morning jumps off the rope swing into the pond and kayak fishing for the guys; nice, relaxed, slow morning risings from caretakers Erika and Shannon … can you picture it? It was like a little piece of heaven.

Highlights were Deb's amazing appetite, her good, restful sleep, her ability to still jet ski slowly—with only one good arm, hammock naps, heart-to-heart talks (both laughter and tear filled), watching our teens play the days away, Guesstures at night, and a fabulous fireworks display over the pond thanks to Dave and the two boys.

At times, sadness would rise up, bringing both Jen and me to tears. Our emotions were always so close to the surface as we watched Deb battle her pain so courageously. These are some of the moments I witnessed:

- The wishful look on her face as she watched Jen and I sail off the rope and into the water.
- Deb take her turn at Guesstures, performing better than the rest of us with only one good arm.
- Her sleeping so peacefully with her arm elevated high.
- The unforgettable beauty of Deb and her two daughters lying together on the hammock.
- The look of love that would light up her face when Dave came up behind her and wrapped his arms around her.

I am weepy picturing "our Deb" in heaven because I miss her so. The reality of all that she is experiencing is making me smile through my tears. I like to picture her swimming in a sea of glassy beauty, then shattering that surface with a Tarzan yell and cannonball splash off a long rope swing; feeling the wind as she jet skis full speed across a warm pond by day, and kayaking with the Lord and the loons some golden evenings."

During the weekend, Deb told us a story that she had shared with her children, as she prepared them for the possibility of her heading heavenward in the not too distant future. It became very special to the children, and Shannon later read it at her mother's funeral. It goes like this:

The Dragonfly Story

Down below the surface of a quiet pond lived a little colony of water bugs. They were a happy colony, living far away from the sun. For many months they were very busy, scurrying over the soft mud on the bottom of the pond. They did notice that every once in awhile one of their colony seemed to lose interest in going about. Clinging to the stem of a pond lily, it gradually moved out of sight and was seen no more.

"Look!" said one of the water bugs to another. "One of our colony is climbing up the lily stalk. Where do you think she is going?" Up, up, up it slowly went. Even as they watched, the water bug disappeared from sight. Its friends waited and waited, but it didn't return ....

"That's funny!" said one water bug to another. "Wasn't she happy here?" asked a second. "Where do you suppose she went?" wondered a third.

No one had an answer. They were greatly puzzled. Finally, one of the water bugs, a leader in the colony, gathered its friends together. "I have an idea," he said. "The next one of us who climbs up the lily stalk must promise to come back and tell us where he or she went and why."

"We promise," they said solemnly.

One spring day, not long after, the very water bug who had suggested the plan found himself climbing up the lily stalk. Up, up, up he went. Before he knew what was happening, he had broken through the surface of the water and fallen onto the broad, green lily pad above.

When he awoke, he looked about with surprise. He couldn't believe what he saw. A startling change had come to his old body. His movement revealed four silver wings and a long tail. Even as he struggled, he felt an impulse to move his wings. The warmth of the sun soon dried the moisture from the new body. He moved his wings again and suddenly found himself up above the water. He had become a dragonfly!

Swooping and dipping in great curves, he flew through the air. He felt exhilarated in the new atmosphere. By and by the new dragonfly lighted happily on a lily pad to rest. Then it was that he chanced to look below to the bottom of the pond. Why, he was right above his old friends, the water bugs! There they were scurrying around, just as he had been doing some time before.

The dragonfly remembered the promise: "The next one of us who climbs up the lily stalk will come back and tell where he or she went and why." Without thinking, the dragonfly darted down. Suddenly he hit the surface of the water and bounced away. Now that he was a dragonfly, he could no longer go into the water ....

"I can't return!" he said in dismay. "At least I tried, but I can't keep my promise. Even if I could go back, not one of the water bugs would know me in my new body. I guess I'll just have to wait until they become dragonflies, too. Then they'll understand what has happened to me, and where I went."

And the dragonfly winged off happily into its wonderful new world
of sun and air ....

Stickney, D. (1997)

As we were shopping one day in Sunapee, we came across a coffee mug
with a dragonfly on it. Deb bought it for me. Whenever we see dragonflies,
we think of "our Deb" enjoying her wonderful new world, the world we
will share with her someday ... heaven!

At the beginning of the weekend Deb had said she just hoped she
could see a loon before she left. As the weekend continued, no loon was
sighted. The final morning, Linda, Deb, and I went out on the jet ski.
You won't be surprised to hear that our loving Father, creator of all living
things, placed two loons in our path. (Well, it was either God, or Linda's
rendition of the loon mating call!) At any rate, we were able to observe
this pair as we floated on the glassy water, the mountains behind us, the
sun shining down on us, and the glory of the Lord surrounding us. Linda
describes it this way:

> "I was at my cabin in New Hampshire early in July
> listening to the loons call out in the evening. I texted
> Deb and said, 'The loons are calling you to Perkins Pond.'
> She wrote back immediately, 'Tell them I am coming!'
> We booked a date and that was that. Deb was a decisive
> woman of action. Once she set her mind to something,
> nothing could stop her. We planned our trip over a busy
> weekend, a Saturday through a Monday, so the loons were
> lying low due to heavy activity on the pond. By Monday,
> our faithful God sent one of His personal calling cards of
> love to Deb, Jen, and me.

Monday afternoon, Deb was on the jet ski ready to drive us for a last
slow pass of the shoreline before loading it on the trailer and heading home.
We prayed to see and hear the loons call out to Deb. We made our slow
loop of the pond without a sighting and arrived back at our dock. Deb got
off the jet ski and headed up toward the cabin, while Jen and I decided to
make one last fast loop of the pond. We took off and got about a quarter
way around when I saw a loon by the shore in the calm water! Jen turned
around and we tore back to the cabin to get Deb.

> Deb hopped back on and we went slowly toward the loon.
> As we approached, I made one of my infamous loon calls

… and surprisingly, the loon answered back! Then to our shock and amazement, another loon near the island to our right called out as well. The loon couple (and I) continued our calls until they both were closely swimming toward each other. We sat there watching them, listening to their haunting calls with the beauty of Mt Sunapee behind them. We were in awe of them, the moment, and our awesome God who loves and gives such perfect gifts from above. Oh, how He intimately loves you and me. We silently watched for a while, and then slowly headed back to the cabin, in total silence, just taking in the hugeness of God's love for us all in that simple, but beautiful gift."

A couple of weeks later found us on our way to the Adirondacks. We stopped at Saratoga Springs Racetrack. It was breast cancer awareness day at the track. Deb was very weak as we entered the grounds, but she trudged along with her husband's help. We could tell it was a force of will for her to be there that day. She loved to please her husband and her children above all else on earth. She so wanted to be strong that day. We had a fun day, and most of us were "up" a couple dollars when we left. I was pretty proud of my $5.00 win! It was exciting to watch those beautiful animals, but we couldn't stay too long. It became obvious that Deb needed to rest. The guys were pulling together some last minute details, so Linda and I went to get the car to pull it up so that Deb didn't have to walk back to it.

Deb walked to the curb with my daughter Emily, her daughter Shannon, and Linda's son Sean. Emily and Sean received another gift from Deb that day: the gift of compassion and strength in tough circumstances. As they were waiting there for the car, in full daylight, and with lots of people around, Deb became very nauseated and threw up all over the sidewalk. They ran for towels and managed to get out a bag for the next round. Then, they gently cleaned her up. I know this impacted my daughter greatly in positive ways. Experience is a fabulous teacher. In fact, my fifteen-year-old daughter wrote this essay to express her feelings.

An Influential Woman

The women in a person's life can influence how they are molded and cause them to become who they are meant to be. Many people have a relative, or maybe just a celebrity that they look up to for inspiration. A woman I admired greatly was Deb O'Donnell, a family friend. Deb inspired me through her joy, love, and faith.

A quality that I admire is true joy, something that shines through a person and makes you happy just being around them. Deb was a cancer victim that was shocked with news of stage four-breast cancer that was terminal. She never let her life become depressing, and realized that every one of us is 'terminal' and she was still going to live life to the fullest. This mind set inspired me to think of my life as terminal, and that I could die any day also. This joyful attitude you cultivate inward turns outward, and people start to want to be around you and want to be joyful, too. She lived life with no boundaries and let happiness and joy lead the way, a concept she imprinted on everyone who really got to know her. She changed my life by helping me see the positive things rather than the negative things in a situation; this made me a generally more joyful person.

Being a loving person and having a genuine love for living is a key component in a happy life. I have always seen people who were very happy in life, but after witnessing somebody who was in agonizing pain through her body night and day and still loved life and loved others regardless of her circumstances, was life changing. My family and Deb's family all went to Nantucket as a wish of Deb, which was part of her bucket list. Everyone wanted to go on the bikes, but Deb could neither pedal nor use her left arm. She, out of her love for us and her love to live life to the fullest, balanced on the back of a two person bike with one hand. She loved us and wanted us to have fun! She loved every minute of it and commented the whole bike ride on how great and beautiful it was. This type of way to look at life, the type of way that allows you to appreciate and love every minute of our small life here on this planet, made me so much more happy doing everyday things that I can take advantage of because of my health. The love she demonstrated throughout her life, especially in her last months, was so powerful that being around her inner and outer beauty could make your love for life and your love for others skyrocket. Love can change a person's outlook on life, as it surely changed mine.

Having faith in God is part of the reason we are here. Faith is what gets us through every day. I felt somewhat independent when it came to turning to someone else to have faith in, but then Deb showed me what security you have when you put one hundred percent of your faith in God. Deb never doubted God's plan; her faith in God to take care of everything in her life was so refreshing to me. She always said that only God knew when she would die, and no doctor or any body else could tell her when she would be dying. She proved all of her doctors wrong by outliving what they told her was her time frame. She inspired me to stop putting all my trust in myself and allowing God to take the burden of having to deal with everything on my own off my shoulders. Before that time, I was not turning to God to ease the stress in my life— until I had a problem where I needed to do something. I got a Bible from my house and opened it up and it led me to exactly what I needed to know. I felt so relieved. Every time I felt down from then on I turned to faith in God, and as my faith grew I felt mentally stronger. I began to get over all these small problems and think about my life as a grain of sand on the beach of eternity, realizing and acknowledging that this life will be over in the blink of an eye and faith in God would make my life so much better. Faith is a tremendous thing especially when you have God to never let you down.

Having joy, love, and faith in your life forms you into a better person. I am so lucky to have had time with Deb before she entered the kingdom of God. Deb was truly one of the most influential people the world has ever seen, and I strive to be more like her.

The day following her difficulties at Saratoga Springs, Deb was back up and ready for action. All I could think of was the quote: "You can knock her down, but you can't knock her out." She dragged branches out of the woods for the evening campfire, took a walk on the shore, allowed us to paddle her about in a blow-up kayak, and yes, even jet-skied behind her daughter. We had a blessed time in the woods and on the water, and also during our quiet, early morning study times on the screen porch with all the adults together.

While we were there, Deb planned for us to come back for a women's weekend the next month in September. She invited twenty plus women to her tiny cabin, bought fall decorations and candles, planned activities and back massages, and gathered family and friends from near and far. During our lives we connect with people from all the places we have grown up, gone to school, and lived out our lives. An eclectic collection of Deb's women friends congregated together that weekend in her tiny … and did I mention tiny … cabin. Bonded by one purpose—loving Deb—we put aside our own agendas, found a bunk, or blew up a mattress and settled in. Her desire was for us to have church on Sunday on her large deck overlooking the stunning lake, with a backdrop of the mountains. Some of her friends were on her "salvation" list. She so wanted all of them to spend eternity with her in heaven, and she overflowed with the love of Christ as she shared what he had done and continued to do in her life. "For I fully expect and hope that I will never be ashamed, but that I will continue to be bold for Christ, as I have been in the past. And I trust that my life will bring honor to Christ, whether I live or die. For to me, living means living for Christ, and dying is even better." Philippians 1:20–21 NLT

Our dear friend Kirsten Locke is a songwriter and worship leader. She led us in song on the deck that September morning. Deb asked her to play "I Will Rise" by Chris Tomlin. She had asked Kirsten to play this at her funeral and we knew that she had asked. Singing it that morning with Deb was indescribable. We knew that the time was coming when we would be apart. It made us sad, but, the joy we felt amid the sadness was truly beyond *my* ability to express it. These verses from Paul's "joy letter" became very real to us. "Above all, you must live as citizens of heaven, conducting yourselves in a manner worthy of the good news about Christ. Then, whether I come and see you again or only hear about you, I will know that you are standing together with one spirit and one purpose, fighting together for the faith, which is the good news. Don't be intimidated in any way by your enemies. This will be a sign to them that they are going to be destroyed, but that you are going to be saved, even by God himself. For you have been given not only the privilege of trusting in Christ but also the privilege of suffering for him. We are in this struggle together. You have seen my struggle in the past, and you know that I am still in the midst of it." Phil 1: 27–30

We were learning deeply the differences between happiness and joy. Joy is magnificent.

Chapter Nine

"The Pilgrim they laid in a large upper chamber, facing the sun-rising. The name of the chamber was Peace." —from Bunyan's *Pilgrim's Progress*

Today is October 20, 2010. It has been a year since we first heard the news of Deb's cancer. My day started out by taking my daughter to school. I planned to go canoeing with Deb and a couple other friends by mid-morning. My daughter had informed me that we were down to one hay bale left for our two horses so I buzzed over to the local farm to pick up a few more bales to carry us over until our next delivery. I lugged five fifty-pound bales into my Range Rover and then out again into the barn when I got home. I rushed in the house, did my breakfast dishes, made spaghetti sauce and meatballs for dinner, threw a load of laundry in, and collected the rubber boots and warm layers required for comfort while paddling on an October afternoon in New England.

The three ladies picked me up about half an hour behind schedule. It seems they had had busy mornings as well. It was now nearing lunchtime, so we stopped at a local diner on the way to the pond where we were headed for our paddle. Deb was at the point where she needed help getting up out of the car, and we heaved her skinny body up out of the car seat. This sounds like an oxymoron, but as her cancer spread she had become very stiff and heavy. Always ready to laugh, she dryly asked us to please try not to break anything during the process. As we walked in the restaurant I asked Deb where she would like to sit. She pointed to a table and said "I'd like to sit right here." Our dear friend Linda cheerily said "No! We need to sit in a booth!" As we headed toward an open booth, Deb, in her deadpan humorous way commented, "I guess I don't get to sit where I want. We are sitting wherever *Linda* wants." Deb had a fantastic sense of humor and never stopped making us laugh no matter how bad things got.

During our lunch she shared the results of her recent PET scan. The cancer had shrunk in her chest area, but had spread in many other places, including her bones. She had been experiencing a lot more pain in her back and legs. Now we knew why. She looked at us and said, "I'm going to die. They've given me until Christmas-time." With that announcement, the waitress came over. We somehow ordered our lunch; Deb got butternut squash ravioli with a garlic cream sauce. As I had so many times before, I marveled at how any of us could think of eating at a time like this. But, following Deb's lead, we ordered our food. The subject got put on hold as one interruption followed another. We did talk about things a little, but not with the kind of depth Deb was seeking. With our stomachs full and our hearts spilling over with every different emotion you can imagine, we headed to Ramani's cabin.

Our friend, Ramani, has a cute little cabin on a pond in the middle of the woods. We pulled up, popped some stuffed apples in to bake, put the coffee on, and hopped into the canoe. Well, not exactly. First, we got Deb a little seat with a back, wrapped her up in blankets, tucked pillows behind her aching back, and then gingerly stepped in ourselves ... careful not to tip the boat or jar her sore body in any way. Ramani had a found a little seat for Deb to sit upon. Linda was in the front and I was in the back. The day was a bit overcast, but lovely just the same. The New England colors were a few days past their peak in our area. I like that. I like it when there are leaves on the ground to crunch under foot, and I like how the colors on the ground add to the beauty of the landscape. As we floated and chatted, suddenly the boat listed heavily to the right! Panicking, I opened my legs to steady the canoe. Had I been paying attention? Did I hit something, or steer too hard that direction? These were the thoughts running through my head. It turns out "our Deb" had fallen asleep! Thankfully, she woke as she felt herself falling over and Ramani was able to catch her. After that, Ramani kept two hands on our friend, just in case she drifted off again. We all had a good laugh, including Deb, who is never afraid to laugh at herself. It struck me as wonderful that she was so comfortable and happy despite the bad news lurking in the back of all our minds, that she could drift off as we made our way along the water bank.

Back in the cabin, we plopped huge spoonfuls of vanilla ice cream on our baked apples, and poured ourselves steaming cups of much anticipated hot drinks. It was chilly out there on the water! As Deb sunk into her chair she blurted, "Okay, come here. We need to pray. Get the Bible." We each had taken about two bites of our apples. We sipped a sip of our coffee. Looking us in the eyes she said, "The trouble is, I don't know how to die. I don't want to die, but I'm going to die." Tears were streaming down her cheeks and her lips were trembling. Our apples forgotten, we gathered closer and laid our hands on hers. We had no words to offer. The symphony was now in a minor key, and we could hear the strains of the music as the notes warred with each other, striking chords that seemed off-key, but were, in fact, freeing in their discord. She went on. "I know I should be praying all day, each day, but I'm not. I know I should be on my knees, but I'm not." This was grieving her deeply. Ramani answered: "Don't you think God understands that, Deb?" More silence as we all grappled with this significant moment we found ourselves in. It was hard to come to terms with the fact that this woman that was so full of life, who just stepped out of a canoe, who was co-leading a Bible study that she envisioned, who always looked stunningly beautiful, who had three lovely children and a husband at home, who was a competitor and had given cancer the kick in the butt it deserved for a whole year, was not going to be with us much longer on earth. It was surreal. "We must keep our focus on the Truth, on eternity and not on our circumstances," Ramani encouraged. We opened *Streams in the Desert,* a devotional book by L.B. Cowman and read the entry for that day. "And the peace of God, which transcends all our powers of thought, will be a garrison to guard your hearts and minds in Christ Jesus" (Phil 4:7). As we read through other Scriptures that Deb had highlighted in her Bible in the book of Philippians, the peace that passes understanding began to creep over us. In time, and after much discussion, we fell into prayer. We thanked God for ... well ... just about everything. Mostly, I felt thankful for the miracle that He had allowed us to witness. The miracle is love. The miracle is the body of Christ coming together for such a time as this, just as He has instructed us to do.

Chapter Ten

"Therefore, I urge you, brothers, in view of God's mercy, to offer your bodies as living sacrifices, holy and pleasing to God—this is your spiritual act of worship" (Romans 12:1).

October 26, 2010. Deb is failing quickly. Today she ate nothing. She took a few spoonfuls of chocolate milkshake, her favorite. Ninety-nine percent of her day she was out of it. Her words were gibberish. The cancer has become the bigger part of her body. It is obstructing her mind, her ability to breathe, and her use of her limbs. Several of her bones have broken. Her ribs, her wrist, and her foot have fractured, and she is on so much pain medication, she hardly knows it.

Last night we held our Monday night Bible study at her home. The week before we decided that we would meet there because Deb was getting weaker. She thought it might be better to meet at her home where she could rest if necessary. It turned out that this was a good decision. None of us realized last week that this week would mark another huge decline in our friend's health. The doctors, as expected, took her out of all the trials and off her vitamin C treatments. A hospital bed was to be delivered that very evening. Still, when Deb wasn't dozing, she would mumble, "I'm not done yet," or "I don't want that bed in the dining room."

Motherhood is such a powerful instinct. When our babies are placed in our arms, we instantly vow to protect this little one above all else. We recognize their cries in a room of crying babies. As they grow we feel their pain, and as they hurt, we hurt every bit as much as they do. Our intuition senses when they are on the wrong path, and we examine them closely to nudge and guide them back to the straight path. Deb's nature was to be a nurturer. She had raised her own three children and foster-parented several others. Her students that she coached in track tell stories of her going above and beyond her coaching duties to reach into their lives. They knew she truly cared about them as people. "Her children arise and call her blessed; her husband also, and he praises her" (Proverbs 31:28). It is no surprise that Deb was still fighting, still running the race with perseverance until God was ready to take her home. Motherly instinct is hard-wired into our brains!

A capella, together we sang one of Deb's favorite hymns: "How Great Thou Art." Deb's eyes were closed as she soaked in the voices. We laid hands on her and prayed over her and her family. In our study of Philippians 4:8 that evening we learned more about joy. "Recognize that the true you is not your flesh and bones. You are a spiritual being living a temporary human experience—a dress rehearsal for eternity. Why not see yourself as joy filled as God created you to be? Remember that joy is an outward sign of inward faith in God's promises. So, by magnifying the joy God has given you, you also exhibit your faith to others and encourage them." Deb was living out this example *right in front of us*. Surely she was not the body that lay in the chair, broken, weak, and weary. She was the joy filled, God honoring woman that got up each time she was knocked down over the past year. Her faith kept her strong for longer than any doctor thought was possible. She had exceeded all their expectations. As she dozed in the comfy armchair, she listened to every word that was spoken during the study. She jumped in with as much clarity as she could a couple times last evening. "It's the joy I see in you, Diane, that encourages me," said Deb. There was no Diane in the room. We all laughed, and Deb laughed with us and at herself, as she realized that she was referring to the woman who had brought her family dinner that evening. This was a perfect example of her inward faith in God's promises giving her the ability to be joy-filled and thankful. She was so grateful for everything everyone did for her and her family. She would tell us over and over again how blessed she was, how wonderful we were, and how thankful she felt. Despite the facts of her physical decline; her desire to live, motherly instincts, and her patient perseverance were encouraging to the fourteen women in the room that evening in very deep, resonating ways.

October 28, 2010. Yesterday, our friend Chris went to see Deb. Deb was extremely agitated. She could not find comfort. She could not express her needs. She understood what those around her were saying, but the cancer had obstructed the part of her brain that allows her to express herself. Chris had brought a passage from the devotional book *His Princess* by Sheri Rose Shepard to read to Deb:

> My Princess …You will forever be remembered
>
> Your life is a treasure that will bless your children's children! I have chosen you, my princess, to carve out the future for the generations that follow your example. Remember, it's your choices, your character, your love and obedience to Me that will live on long after you are gone from this world. My Spirit will continue to give guidance and hope to all who have watched you live out your call. I have covered everything with My blood and have cleansed you from all sin. I want you to discover the joy and purpose of knowing that not only have I called you, I also will live out this great honor with you and through you. When you walk with Me, the model of your life will be more than a memory; it will leave an indelible mark on the hearts and lives of all who loved you. Even their children's children will be blessed because you loved Me. Love, Your King and your Future.
>
> "Happy are those who delight in doing what he commands. Their children will be successful everywhere; an entire generation of godly people will be blessed. They themselves will be wealthy, and their good deeds will never be forgotten."
>
> (Psalm 112:1–3)

Later in the day, I stopped over with my daughter, Emily, and Linda. Deb and her husband Dave have worked on their back yard for many years. It is gorgeous! A waterfall trickles down a stone terrace into a fish pond, and flowers and shrubs gracefully adorn the sides. Both Deb and Dave grew up on the water in up-state New York, and Deb loves to hear the water run down the waterfall. It brings her peace. Over the course of the year, Dave has made sure that Deb's bed has been moved several times so that she can always hear the music of the water. Now, in the study, she has a perfect view of it through the picture window from her hospital bed. When we walked into the study, we saw Deb's mother, Dee, cradling her daughter. Deb's head rested on her mother's chest and she was rocked too and fro, while Deb's own daughters hovered close by. Erika read from the Bible, and Shannon rubbed her mom's back. What a precious, precious picture we will have in our memories forever.

The three of us gathered round the bed. In time, Deb knew we were there. We were blessed with the opportunity to speak to her and remind her of God's promises. I sang to her while the others kept her as comfortable as possible. She was much calmer than she had been all day, but even still, she was writhing on the bed. She lifted her face as I sang "How Great Thou Art" and "The Old Rugged Cross" among other songs. She tried to stand on her sprained and broken feet. We believe she was lifting her face unto the Lord, and wanted to stand to praise her King. As we left, we told her how much we love her. We received a gift: she clearly said, "I love you" back to us.

This morning God showed his faithfulness once again. Several of us received this text from Deb's oldest daughter, Erika. Erika is eighteen years old. She studies at Messiah College, but was now home. A strong believer and one of her mom's biggest faith champions, she recently had the words "faith eclipses fear" tattooed onto her foot … one of the feet that will continue to bring—and has already brought—the good news to many in her short life! This is what the message said:

> I just want to thank you guys for praying for me and my family and let you know that I have such unexplainable and amazing peace right now. I have been a mess all day, and in the last few hours I've just completely turned around. I realized that my mom is on her way to the most amazing place I can think of, and I'm okay with that! I will miss her incredibly, but I love her way too much to watch her keep suffering and I just know that God can take much better care of her than I ever can! So I love you guys so much and just wanted you to know your prayers are most definitely working! The only explanation for me being so peaceful right now is that God is amazing, and I trust him. We're all going to get through this! Together!

Deb died two days later, on October 30, 2010.

Chapter Eleven

"My soul magnifies the Lord, and my spirit rejoices in God my Savior." (Luke 1:46–47)

March 2011. Last year at this time, Deb was recovering from her double mastectomy. She couldn't be at our Women's Retreat, "Loving Well," because the surgery had just been completed. She desired to be there and longed for the fellowship of her women friends. We made her a rap video during the weekend that made her laugh and laugh when we got together to watch it later the following week. The video made her feel she was with us, even though she was not able to be there in person.

The content of our retreat last year talked about loving well (hence the name!). Beth Moore, as I've already told you earlier in the book, attempted to teach us just what that looked like. We were so blessed to not only have the head knowledge taught to us through her DVDs, but to have a year to learn it "hands on." For this year's retreat, God led us to Beth's DVD series *He Is*. There was no "retreat in a box" to lean on with this four-part series. We searched the web for study notes, or a leader's guide, with no success. I believe God gave us this study because He wanted *us* to study the material deeply and to write our own study guide. He showed us we could do it with His help and guidance.

From my very first review of DVD one, I felt the power in the message. Quickly, I called my team together and commissioned them to pray earnestly over this teaching. The message was intense, real, basic, and so very important. I suspected we would need to gird ourselves like never before as we prepared for retreat. We "swung our swords" as we joyfully set to work planning during the following two months. No surprise, God met us again in an even more powerful way than any of us could have imagined!

Twenty-four women from seven different churches retreated to Cape Cod. After session one, we listened to "our Deb's" testimony, which she had given at her church the prior year. It was bittersweet to hear her voice, recorded while she was still hoping to beat the cancer, but assuring us that even if God didn't give her the miracle of physical healing, He was Sovereign and she would love Him every day of her life. As we listened to her voice, we knew with certainty that she *was in heaven* with God. She was *there*. She had laid her crown at Jesus' feet! She had finished her race. Filled to overflowing with thankfulness for her life and the lessons we were allowed to learn through it, our friend Chris tearfully attempted to sum it up for us. "The Love, the Love, the Love …" was just about all I heard, and all I needed to hear, because that *was* what we learned. The love in listening to each other, in crying together, in praying together; the love in cleaning wounds together, in massaging tired muscles together, in laughing together; the love in sisterhood, and love in studying together. There was love in the Psalm readings, in the hymn singing, in the car-pooling, in the meal-making. There was love in the hugs for Deb, for Dave and the children, for their extended family members, and for each other. There was love in the quilting, in the loon sightings, and in each beautiful face, whether it was worn, teary, smiling, or bowed down. Most of all, there was love in the realization and revelation of the wonderfully different and unique gifts God placed in each us and how, together—and only by working together—we could meet Deb's needs. Chris summed it up perfectly … "the love … 24/7."

This note was just written to us by a woman who had never joined our group before this weekend retreat.

> I am home. I arrived yesterday, late afternoon. I was exhausted, but so fulfilled! This weekend was just what I needed. Twenty-three new and amazing sisters to add to my life. The teaching was intense, and just for me, I'm sure (ha ha)! The testimonies were encouraging and beautiful to hear. God is on the move. I am testimony to that.
>
> One of the most encouraging parts of this weekend was the fact that the women were transparent and willing to share their personal walk with Jesus. Not one bit of gossip, cattiness, no tempers lost, nothing artificial about

it. Just complete unity from twenty-four different women from completely different walks of life, representing seven different churches. I was amazed! The one thing we all had in common? Our desire for more of Jesus in us.

We discovered much about who He is ... and who we are in Him. I was in the company of women who are seeking Him as ardently as I am. I can't relay enough how encouraged and refreshed I am! I am ready to continue my journey with even more fervency. He is drawing the church to Himself and it is evident that something huge is happening!

I am convinced; it is through the love of Christ, manifested in us by the power of the Holy Spirit, which allows our souls to magnify the Lord. The body of Christ coming together, in tune with the Holy Spirit, under the blood of Christ is surely the Lord's *Opus Magnificat*.

One of the ladies found a metal dragonfly sculpture at a local store and gave it to me as a gift. We took a picture of our whole group that weekend ... and Deb was with us. You'll see her in the middle ... represented by the dragonfly.

"He Is" retreat, March 2011, where Deb's spirit lives on.
(Linda Goehle photo)

Epilogue

It has been a year since Deb walked incredibly strong despite her incredibly weak body in the name of breast cancer research during the Boston Avon Walk for Breast Cancer. It has been five years since she walked it the first time and was handed an "every three minutes" ribbon.

For the past nine years, thousands have crowded the Boston streets proudly wearing pink, walking with their heads held high and wearing backpacks jammed with Band-Aids, water bottles, and snacks. Among them in 2011 were two of Deb's children, her husband, Dave, my daughter Emily, and other family and friends. Their t-shirts proudly proclaimed "Incurable is NOT a declaration, it's a DARE!"—one of Deb's famous quotes. The cheerleaders, of which I was one, shook our pompoms, handed out buttons, and yelled long and loud for the courageous walkers. We had made many signs, some with limericks, others with Scripture, but our favorite sign said "Go Deb's Warriors!" As the walkers read our signs, we found out just how many lives Deb had touched at the 2010 walk.

Repeat walkers came up to our group, and looking into our eyes, asked "Did you know Deb?" They wanted to share how encouraged they were by having met her. At times, with tears in their eyes, they remarked on what an inspiration she had been to them. We were connected by shared grief—and by shared hope for the future of this disease.

We all felt Deb's presence with us during the two-day walk. The rain stopped long enough for the group to walk in comfort until they reached the finish line, and as we turned the last corner onto University Drive, there, in the harbor, was a single loon. We looked at each other, and smiled.

CPSIA information can be obtained at www.ICGtesting.com
Printed in the USA
267712BV00003B/2/P